The Way of Prayer

The Way of Prayer

John Baycroft

Anglican Book Centre
Toronto, Ontario

1983
Anglican Book Centre
600 Jarvis Street
Toronto, Ontario
Canada M4Y 2J6

Printed in Canada

Canadian Cataloguing in Publication Data

Baycroft, John.
  The Way of Prayer
ISBN 0-919030-79-3

1. Prayer.   I. Title.

BV210.2.B38   248.3'2   C82-094105-3

Contents

Introduction

This little book is about how to pray. The only excuse for another book on this subject is that most of the good books seem too complicated. Perhaps those who are more advanced in prayer sometimes forget what novices the rest of us are. My only qualification is that I have never passed beyond the first stages of prayer, where I have been operating for many years. I would like to be able to claim that I live on the lofty peaks of spiritual achievement, but all I can do is write about the lowlands I have learned to love. The advantage of the lowlands of prayer is that we can all reach them. Simple prayer is not to be scorned.

A "how-to-do-it" book is likely to sound dogmatic or else be hopelessly confusing. My approach is to risk the accusation of being dogmatic. I know I cannot turn this aside with a disclaimer, but please try to think of me as a clerk in a shoe store. My job is, as it were, to help you find a pair of shoes that will fit — actually, a way of praying that will suit you. I may say, "Try this!" or "Most people find this style very comfortable." But if you go out in pain and come back with blisters, you ought not to blame the clerk. There are lots of shoes in the store, and you are the only person who can decide whether or not they fit you. Please understand that all my suggestions are tentative. Of course all the shoes are useless unless you are willing to use the power God gives you to walk with him.

I am searching for a sane spirituality that will make the experience of the past and the insights of the present accessible to ordinary Christians. My approach is practical but the underlying theory is theological. For that reason I begin with the gospel teaching and end with the doctrine of the Holy Trinity. Along the way simple theological reflections are interspersed with the practical suggestions. I believe that a grasp of the theological underpinnings of prayer allows us to experiment freely and confidently, neither rigid prisoners of the suggested method nor defenceless victims of any exotic idea that momentarily captures our imagination.

Without any doubt the most valuable thing we can learn about prayer is that God is always accessible — in the lowlands as readily as on the mountain tops. I believe the next most valuable thing is to learn to persevere. There are a few other tips in the rest of the book which I hope you will find helpful.

1   Lord, teach us to pray

When his disciples asked Jesus to teach them to pray, he taught them. The story of this incident in Saint Luke's Gospel makes it sound almost too easy. Yet if prayer is as important for the Christian life as the Church has always taught, then it must be possible for ordinary people to learn how to do it. Before outlining a very simple way to pray, it will be helpful to look at some of the basic New Testament teaching on prayer, restricting ourselves to the verses immediately before and after the incident in Luke's Gospel when Jesus teaches the disciples the Lord's Prayer. This passage is Luke 10:21 to 11:13.

Luke does not give us pages from a diary describing the life of Jesus. Instead, with the skills of a careful theologian and the gifts of a talented artist, he does the work of an evangelist. Luke meticulously arranges teachings, incidents, people's reactions to our Lord, and the major events of the story of Jesus Christ, so that we come to understand and believe the good news which is the gospel. Like a painter selecting and arranging colours, he chooses each part of his Gospel to complement what precedes and follows it. So it is not surprising that we learn a lot about prayer from the passages before and after the Lord's Prayer.

One of the most important lessons in the New Testament is that Jesus prayed. If he needed to pray and showed us that example, then it is not likely that we shall get very far in trying to follow him, or succeed in becoming Christ-like, unless we also pray. Luke 10:21 describes a high point in Jesus's ministry. The seventy missionaries whom he had sent out two by two returned to our Lord with accounts of the power of the gospel. In his prayer at this time Jesus "rejoiced in the Holy Spirit" and thanked his Father for revealing things to those who are simple. There follow some profound words on the relationship of the Father and the Son. The meaning of verse twenty-two becomes clearer as we practise prayer ourselves and experience Christ, the Son, revealing the Father to us. Next Jesus turned to the disciples and privately said, "Blessed are the eyes which see what you see . . ." A privilege of discipleship is to see and hear what was not even granted to the prophets. The modern disciple continues to receive God's revelation in prayer.

Luke's story continues with a lawyer asking, "What shall I do to inherit eternal life?" This is a basic question about what really matters in life. When all that is trivial or temporary or merely relatively important is taken away, what really counts is what the New Testament calls "eternal life." How then do we find it? Jesus asked the lawyer to give his understanding of what God had already revealed in the law and the prophets which were available for all to read in the Scriptures. Jesus agreed with the lawyer's answer that love is what really counts in this life. Loving is the way to eternal life.

The two commandments of the Gospel do not, however, refer to a vague or abstract love, but to loving God actively and completely, and love for our neighbour. Prayer is one of the ways in which the love of God is actually experienced by human beings. When the lawyer asked a supplementary question about the love of our neighbour, Jesus replied with the parable of the good Samaritan, giving an example of concrete loving action. Notice that when we are thinking at the most basic level of what really matters, the two loves — of God and neighbour — are inseparable. So in the Christian life today prayer and service to others belong together. This book is about prayer, but it can only make sense in the context of the whole Christian life which also includes the other dimension of service.

Next Luke whisks us off to Martha's house, and we have a similar point made by a short but highly suggestive story. Martha was busy making a great fuss over the preparation of a feast for her favourite guest, while her sister Mary sat at Jesus's feet and listened to his ''word'' or teaching. Understandably Martha protested. Perhaps Jesus merely meant by his reply that Martha was going to too much trouble with too many dishes, and that "just a cup of tea" would have been sufficient, although no doubt he intended to do justice to the delicious dinner. He was certainly not contemptuous toward Martha the worker, and on another occasion (John 11) he talked with her at the very deepest theological and spiritual level about the Resurrection. But this time he made it clear that he came for the visit, not the victuals, and that Mary had chosen the "good portion."

It is not fanciful to see here a contrast of two ways of loving — both important — but the first of very limited value without the second. Martha's love is the love that does things for the loved one. This is the first love of service. Mary's love is the love that is content to be with the loved one. Instead of giving service she gives herself. Of course service is important, but we can all remember with regret occasions when well intentioned busyness has prevented us from sharing ourselves. There is a difference between giving our lives for a cause or a person and giving ourselves to someone. The first love is essential because it leads to right action, righteousness, justice, service, and kindness. Without these we cannot survive and remain truly human. Yet noble as it is, it is an incomplete love if it lacks the dimension of giving oneself to the other. The second love, when directed toward God, leads to giving ourselves to him and sharing his life — to communion, mystical union, and holiness. This love also is essential if we are to fulfil our human potential. Prayer is a way of being with our Lord and giving ourselves to him. It is the good portion that Jesus would not allow to be taken away from Mary.

At the beginning of chapter eleven Luke tells us of Jesus praying again. Then one of his disciples asked him to teach them to pray, as John the Baptist had taught his disciples. Probably the request was for some distinctive or agreed words which they could use together as a form of corporate prayer. As is usually the case with grace, they got far more than they asked for. They were taught words that Christians around the world and throughout the centuries have continued to use, and they learned the normative model for all Christian prayer. St Thomas Aquinas quotes with approval St Augustine's words, "If we pray rightly and fittingly, we can say nothing else but what is contained in the Lord's Prayer" (*Summa Theologiae*, 2a2ae, 83.9, vol. 39, Blackfriars, p. 71). We do well to pray the Lord's Prayer frequently, slowly, and thoughtfully. It invites volumes of comments, yet it can speak simply for itself.

After the Lord's Prayer we find a humorous parable about prayer. If something is important, we ought not to give up easily. In a house with only one bedroom and perhaps only one bed, a neighbour banging on the door in the middle of the night is a nuisance. But if he keeps on banging and the children are going to wake up anyway, you might just as well get up and give him what he wants. Jesus is teaching us to persevere when we pray. We ought not to be quickly discouraged. In fact, he made the amazing promise, "Ask and it will be given you; seek and you will find; knock and it will be opened" (Luke 11:9).

But before we can be misled into thinking that prayer is some form of magic or manipulation, in which we can pester God into giving us our own way, Luke introduces another of Jesus's parables. Speaking of fathers and sons, our Lord reminds us that parents do not give their children what is bad for them. If imperfect human beings give good gifts to their children, how much more will the heavenly Father give what is good to us his children. Notice, however, one of Jesus's typical surprises in the tail of this parable. Instead of promising that the Father will give us literally whatever we ask, he says that the Father will give the Holy Spirit to those who ask him. In other words, what we are guaranteed in prayer is not that we shall be given our own way, nor even what we most desperately desire and sincerely believe we need; the promise is that God will give himself to us. This lesson is underlined later in the Gospel in Luke 22:42. In agony on the Mount of Olives, Jesus prayed, "Remove this cup from me."

Although we know that he had to drink that cup on the cross, we would be mistaken if we believed that his prayer was not answered. Jesus prayed, "Father, *if thou art willing*, remove this cup from me; nevertheless *not my will, but thine, be done.*" This prayer of our Lord, "thy will be done," is included in the form of the Lord's Prayer with which we are most familiar (from the Sermon on the Mount — Matthew 6:8-13). This qualification is implicit in and modifies all Christian prayer. Lest we think it is divine severity, or even a weasel clause to allow the Father to escape from the Son's too rash promise, remember that we are promised better than the satisfaction of our wishes. God's commitment to us and his purpose is to be united with us and give himself, the Holy Spirit, to all who approach him in prayer.

In thirty-five verses Luke has given us a careful introduction to, an enlightening context for, and a concise summary of, Jesus's teaching on prayer. If you have been reading Luke's Gospel, as well as skimming over these pages, I hope you have decided that the Bible has a lot more to teach you. In the following chapters we shall not overload the text with biblical references; but please remember that we began with the New Testament and the Gospel because that is where our understanding of Christian prayer is rooted. It is very important that we learn from the Bible that Jesus prayed to and thanked the

Father and rejoiced in the Holy Spirit, that God reveals his word and himself to simple disciples, that we know the way to eternal life, that the love of God and love of our neighbour are insperable and unconditional imperatives, and that service is essential, but that communion, communication with God — prayer — is the better part. The Lord's Prayer provides a model to guide and test whatever form of prayer we use. Jesus encourages constant and confident prayer, and promises that the Father will give us the Holy Spirit.

2　A simple method

My grandfather was a likeable old rascal who twice survived the demolition of his house by Hitler's bombs. On the second occasion, he and his lady friend had neglected to go to the air raid shelter. When they realized that the house was coming down, they squeezed together under the kitchen table, and grandfather, who only attended church for unavoidable weddings or funerals, said, "Polly, we should say a prayer!" To which she replied, "Yes John, do you know one?" Apparently neither of them did. At some time or other almost everyone feels the desire to pray, but many are thwarted because they do not know where to start.

Prayer is conversation with God, and there is no single way that is the only right way to conduct a conversation. The suggestions that follow here are only one simple method which many Christians have found helpful in getting started on the way of prayer.

Step one is to close our eyes and remember that we are in God's presence. At this stage in the conversation we do not need to say anything. Just being glad he is with us is enough. If we say anything, it should be about God.

The second step is to think about ourselves without forgetting God's presence. When we think of ourselves in the presence of God, we shall inevitably

17

become conscious of our shortcomings and unworthiness. Since this feeling is a nuisance in our conversation with God, the best thing to do is deal with it systematically. So the second stage of this simple method is to confess our sins to God, confident, of course, that he will forgive us.

Although I feel that the third step is the least important, I know that it is often what stimulates people to pray. It is the most widespread form of prayer and the part least likely to be forgotten. This is petition. Petition is that part of the conversation in which we ask God to do something for us or for others.

Regrettably, thanksgiving, the fourth step, is easy to forget. A conversation without an expression of gratitude when there is so much for which we can say thank you, is a poor way to relate to God.

The final step should be to form a resolution, and before we leave the conversation we ought to make a commitment to God to do what we have resolved. This we call dedication.

The five ingredients of prayer are adoration, penitence, petition, thanksgiving, and dedication. When arranged in a sequence of five steps as above, these ingredients become a simple pattern for prayer. Following this pattern is a well tried method of prayer, equally suited to the needs of the beginner and the experienced Christian. It is easily learned and will not be quickly discarded. It wears well with lots of room for growth.

The first thing we have to do is find some time. Anyone who is serious about prayer will be willing to commit at least five to ten minutes a day. But which five minutes? The trick is to choose the time that you feel you are most likely to be able to protect. It is not that occasional interruptions really matter much in themselves. We can always start again or pick up from the point at which we were disturbed. But we need to feel that we are probably not going to be interrupted so that we can relax, stop bothering about externals, and keep our minds more or less concentrated. We also need to have our bodies in a comfortable position. It helps if the spine is erect. Any quiet place is a good location.

Having found a time, a place, and a comfortable position we need to let ourselves know that we have started our prayer. The ancient invocation, "In the name of the Father, and of the Son, and of the Holy Spirit," is a good beginning. Without bothering about exact timing, we keep the first two minutes of our prayer for adoration. In order to do this we simply think about God. You may object that it is not always easy to think about God. But remember — God loves us and comes to us even when our minds refuse to rest on him. We are in his presence, and in this conversation he is the partner who is going to do most of the work. Our main responsibility is to be there. It may help to imagine a natural scene that evokes a sense of wonder, beauty, power, or tranquillity. We may choose a biblical scene such as Isaiah's vision in the temple from the Old Testament, or the Crucifixion from the Gospel. Or you may recreate in your mind the setting and occasion of one of your peak experiences of worship. The aim is to use a mental picture to create a reverent frame of mind and, through our sense of wonder, love, beauty, grace, and glory, to focus our attention on the living God who elicits these responses.

Our mind is only briefly occupied with the picture, which is merely a tool to take our thoughts away from the jumble of mundane concerns and lift them to God in whose presence we are and to whom the picture points. This is not a relaxation exercise in which we admire the scenery, but an aid to the realization that we are indeed in contact and in conversation with our heavenly Father, who is the creator and source of all that is. The more God reveals himself to us, and the better we get to know him, the greater will be our adoration. Our wonder and excitement increase as we discover not only the overawing dimensions of his power and holiness, but also the gentleness, graciousness, and humility in which he approaches us. For other people music might be more effective than visual stimulation. Recall some beautiful music which has turned your mind to God in the past, recreate the sound in your mind, and let it help you become aware of the reality of God's presence with you again.

The use of a lot of words in the two minutes of adoration is to be avoided. If you feel a need for words, then try to make sure that at this stage they are about God. For example, you might use the Gloria, ''Glory to the Father, and to the Son, and to the Holy Spirit: as it was in the beginning, is now, and will be for ever.'' If you choose this way, my advice is to use the same few words slowly and repeatedly. Occasionally it is a good idea to dwell on the meaning of each word carefully. The point of this step is to find ourselves enjoying the presence of God and worshipping him. It is enough to be with him, allowing any words simply to flow through our consciousness and carry us into an awareness of God. For adoration helpful words can be drawn from hymns of praise, from psalms and canticles in the Prayer Book, from prayer anthologies, or from your own spontaneous words. There are some suggestions in the appendix to this book (page 104). Only use as many as you need. We do not want our chatter to get in the way of our awareness of God himself.

The next step is penitence. In our daily prayer this ought not to be prominent, but it must not be neglected or avoided. On occasion we need to do a thorough examination of our lives, and this will take longer than the time available in our regular quiet time. In a short daily prayer of five to ten minutes, one minute should suffice for self examination, confession, and a prayer for forgiveness. We let the mind, which has been dwelling on God, turn back to ourselves and see our lives through his eyes. Conscious of his closeness, and aware that he sees into the depths of our being, we try to examine our feelings about what we have been doing, thinking, and saying in our daily lives. We include, of course, our feelings about what we have not done. We need to be specific. If there is some particular action of which we are ashamed, we should acknowledge it and avoid excuses. When we recognize a persistent or habitual fault, we should not merely deplore it but determine with God's help to change.

The gospel teaches with crystal clarity that God wants to forgive us when we repent, so we can be completely confident that he hears us lovingly. Jesus also teaches that, if we ask forgiveness, we must be prepared to be forgiving. We cannot turn prayer into a private affair between God and ourselves, because our attitudes to others must be consistent with our relationship with God. In our century some thoughtful Christians are of the opinion that previous generations, particularly in the Western church, wallowed too much in guilt and grovelled excessively in their devotion. Nevertheless, without encouraging any unhealthy exploitation of guilt feelings, we need to become penitents before we can escape the bondage of the past and be free to live up to our present and future potential.

Asking for forgiveness leads naturally into the next step in the method of prayer. In petition we bring all of our requests to God. Some people use a written "shopping list" so that they do not forget any person for whom they want to pray but remember all of the things that they feel they need to ask. Others simply let their concerns surface in their minds and present them to God. In this free flow approach we find that we remember the things that are most important to us, and these are the subjects about which we need to talk to God. If you are like me, you will often find that you cannot decide what you want to ask. For example, if you are watching a person suffering and close to death, you may not know whether to ask that they be restored to physical health or that they die peacefully. You only know that you want to hold them in God's presence and put their need and your helplessness in his loving care. Thinking this in God's presence is prayer and petition enough. On other occasions you know exactly what you want. In that case it is appropriate to ask directly, always remembering that whether you are absolutely convinced that what you are asking is right, or have the sinking feeling even as you ask that it may be wrong, all petitions are qualified by the petition "thy will be done."

No subject matter is illegitimate in prayer if it is important to us. Personally I cannot get enthusiastic about instructing the almighty in appropriate ways to interfere in his universe. I do, however, believe that it is natural and right for us to want to talk to God about all the needs of society, of other persons, and of ourselves. God's care for us is even greater, and the bond between us more intimate, than we could find in the best relationship of a parent with children. God is inseparably involved in all that is; so talking with him about anything at all will help us. The Prayers of the People in the Eucharist will give you some idea of the wide range of concerns that ought to find a place in our petitions, as well as more private and less easily articulated thoughts that we might hesitate to express publicly.

If we ask ourselves how we feel in our relationship with God, one of our answers will probably be that we feel thankful. If we ask what we believe we ought to feel, we shall certainly answer that we ought to be thankful. The fourth step of thanksgiving expresses an essential dimension of our relationship with God. By doing it daily in our prayers we help to maintain a right relationship. In the Eucharist we bless God for who he is and thank him for what he does, and in our daily prayers we continue these activities. We do not express gratitude because we believe that God likes to be flattered. We need to say thank you far more than God needs to hear it said. We can often feel our mood change, our joy increase, and our confidence grow as we move into this stage of thanksgiving. Not least among the causes of our thankfulness is the knowledge of God's presence with us and our personal contact with him as we say thank you. As with confession and petition, thanksgiving should also be specific. Very general expressions of gratitude become pious platitudes only too easily.

The fifth step of dedication is often omitted because it is considered implicit in the other four parts of prayer. I believe we ought to make it explicit at the end of our time of prayer. Sometimes we may have to be satisfied with a very general resolution to follow Christ more closely. But our aim ought to be to make our resolution very specific. When we have been talking with God for about five minutes, during which time we have been listening as well as speaking, and when the conversation has been about important matters in our lives, we shall frequently have a strong feeling that God wants us to do something. It may be that we resolve to write a letter, to attempt a reconciliation, to make a gift, to stop talking so much, or to give up smoking. The potential list is endless. We discern something definite and then make a commitment to God to do it, confident in his help. This promise is not the only way in which our daily prayer will influence our daily lives, but it is one way to ensure that there is a genuine connection there. It will help to keep us honest when we pray "thy will be done."

If our quiet time is in the morning, we can conclude by saying, "I will go forth in the name of Christ. Thanks be to God." In the evening it would be more appropriate to say, "Into thy hands, O Lord, I commend my spirit." At any time we can use the words, "The grace of our Lord Jesus Christ, and the love of God, and the fellowship of the Holy Spirit, be with us evermore."

Regular use of this method will make it feel comfortable. Since we do it on our own with God, we can be very free and flexible in mixing and arranging the five ingredients. You may be encouraged to modify the pattern if you examine the public prayers of the church. There you will discover all five parts present but rarely in separate compartments. Feel free to experiment. Good communication between lovers ought not to become rigid.

A loose leaf note book can be made into your own personal prayer book. On five separate pages write the five headings: Adoration, Penitence, Petition, Thanksgiving, and Dedication. Under each heading write the words of any form of prayer you find helpful. Examples are given in the appendix (page 104 to 112). Change these prayers from time to time, and build up a collection. Keep blank pages in the book, and have a pencil handy when you pray. You will be amazed at how many important insights flash into your mind in prayer, and how hard it often is to remember them afterwards. Writing a note is not much of an interruption in the time of prayer and is of great benefit later. If, however, you do find that this is distracting, then try to record your insights as soon as possible after your quiet time. Of course, you ought not to become tied to the note book. An advantage of this form of prayer is that it allows us to fly free. Just close your eyes and soar.

3   Why pray?

Knowing why we pray helps us to pray. First, the reasons for prayer will provide clues and insights into how to pray. Secondly, we are more likely to persevere when we know why we are doing something. True prayer is a relationship which lasts for ever, and in this life at least a permanent relationship requires perseverance.

Christians want to follow Jesus and become Christ-like. In the Gospels we read that our Lord prayed frequently both in public worship and in private prayer. We pray because of this example.

At a deeper and more internal level we pray because by baptism we are each a part of the body of Christ. From the New Testament we learn that Jesus not only prayed during his earthly ministry but also that as the risen and glorified Christ, at the right hand of God, he indeed intercedes for us (e.g. Romans 8:34, Hebrews 7:25). To probe into the meaning of this heavenly intercession would require an attempt to describe the internal relations of the divine Persons in the Holy Trinity. This would show how deeply prayer is rooted in the nature of God. Here it is sufficient to affirm that we pray because we are caught up in Christ's continuing prayer by virtue of our membership in the Church. The Church has always been quite explicit about this. Christians are expected to pray corporately and individually. If we are truly united with Christ, then we share in what he does, including prayer.

We pray because it is our nature to pray. Although this book deals exclusively with Christian prayer, the reader will be aware that prayer also permeates non-Christian cultures and religions. An over-simplified account of the almost universal phenomenon of prayer would say that human beings pray because it is their natural inclination to do so. The doctrine of creation begins with a personal God. He creates the universe from love and for love. The role of human beings is to be persons who can be loved and love. Furthermore, this love is not merely an activity between human beings for the enjoyment of the divine but distant spectator; God is a partici-pant in the activity of loving. We are created to love God as well as each other, and the personal creator reaches out to us in love. Love requires communion and communication. Lovers converse. Lovers want to be in each others' presence. Being in God's presence and sharing a conversation with our divine creator and lover is prayer. Prayer, therefore, is at the heart of our purpose for being. God made us to pray. The Lord God walking in the garden in the cool of the day beautifully evokes the mood of prayer. But if we remember the whole story, we know that creatures do not remain in perfect communion with the creator, and something has to be done about our alienation if we are to become true to our created nature.

Christian prayer is rooted in the doctrine of redemption as well as in our theology of creation. The biblical story of salvation tells how over and over again the loving creator showed his care for his people. We wander away and allow communication to break down; God reaches out and begins the dialogue again. Supremely in Jesus Christ God accomplishes atonement. This at-one-ment is the original purpose of creation which must not be thwarted. We are made for love with God and to be at-one with him. When we pray, then, we are not only being true to our created nature as humans, we are also expressing our redeemed nature as Christians who experience salvation through the at-one-ing grace of Christ.

As Christians we are members of the Spirit-filled community of the Church, and God has given himself, his Holy Spirit, to dwell in each of us, uniting our spirits with his Spirit. Saint Paul wrote, "The Spirit helps us in our weakness; for we do not know how to pray as we ought, but the Spirit himself intercedes for us with sighs too deep for words. And he who searches the hearts of men knows what is the mind of the Spirit" (Romans 8:26, 27). We pray because it is our spiritual nature to do so.

The experience of lovers in each other's company, and the conversation that takes place between them, has special characteristics differing from other interpersonal relationships. Because prayer is a love relationship, it includes a deep sharing of concerns. We do not only tell God what is worrying us, we are also open to becoming aware of God's concerns and plans for his world and for us. Lovers exchange vows, and in prayer we make our resolutions and commitments to God and put our trust in his promises to us. Lovers cooperate, and cooperation requires communication. Prayer includes seeking and receiving guidance, and strength to share in God's creative and redemptive activity in the world. When there is estrangement and injury, a love relationship requires reconciliation. So prayer includes both the expression of repentance and hearing the divine word of forgiveness. Love includes gratitude and thanksgiving. In a love relationship the lovers appreciate each other. We adore God, but we are usually overwhelmed when we realize that he appreciates our worth in spite of our weakness, that he truly cares for us, makes himself available to us, respects us, and values each one of us as if there were only one of us. We pray because we are in a love relationship with God.

Because prayer is an activity of love, it cannot be reduced to a cosy and comfortable private relationship between the individual and God. It demands the total giving of the personal self to God in a way that overrides all other concerns. Our love is caught up in the breadth of the divine love. Christian love includes the love of the good Samaritan and Martha following the way of loving service. It includes the love of which Jesus spoke when he said, "Greater love has no man than this, that a man lay down his life for his friends" (John 15:13). It even expands to embrace the love that Jesus demonstrated the day after those words were spoken, when he gave his life for enemies also. This love, which is given for others and which demands concrete loving action, has a place in our prayers. Intercession for others, seeking guidance for loving behaviour, and gaining insight into God's loving purposes, all propel us into active love. This is expressed in personal and social righteousness and justice. Justice depends on right relationships. Prayer is the experience of a right relationship with God and demands a right attitude to others. Prayer is inextricably interwoven with the love that lives in justice.

Prayer as an activity of love also includes the love of Mary. Mary the sister of Martha was commended by Jesus for being with him and giving her whole self to him rather than merely doing something for him. Another Mary, the mother of our Lord, by being receptive fulfilled her role in the world's salvation. By her example of keeping in her heart and pondering those things that she did not yet understand, she showed the way for all subsequent disciples, who have found that the most important part of prayer is to be there and be available with a receptive heart. This is the mystical dimension of prayer which is rooted in the mystical union between Christ and the Church. In prayer we give ourselves to God and he gives himself to us. The rest of the conversations is commentary on this union.

Christians believe that every human being needs to pray. Even if our life were tranquil, and we felt happy and fulfilled, there would still be something lacking if this good life did not allow us to reach beyond the limitations of our finite existence. We fall short of full humanity if we do not transcend our human condition. Because we are made for the love of God, we hunger for the transcendent and spiritual dimension of life and reality. At the other end of the spectrum countless men and women in desperation and at their wits' end cry out in their need for God's salvation. The saint on the mountain top and two sinners huddled under a table as the bombs explode and the roof collapses, equally need to pray. Their circumstances differ in almost every way, but their need for God, and his love for them all, make prayer necessary for them all. God will be present with them, and they all need to turn to him. We pray because we need God.

Some people would want to include the power of prayer as one of the reasons why we pray. We can cautiously admit that prayer gives access to spiritual power, but I do not want to recommend this for reasons that tilt toward an attempt to manipulate God or that hint of magic and superstition. If we become fascinated by the power of prayer, there is a danger that we shall fall into the trap which a wise person described as "coveting the mercies of God when we should be seeking the God of mercies." We seek God in prayer because we need to find him, and he meets us because he made us for this encounter. We ought not to pray because we want to get our hands on his power, although it is all right to put ourselves into his powerful hands.

This Christian approach to why we pray and what prayer is, explains why the five ingredients we listed in the previous chapter are always regarded as essential in traditional Church teaching on prayer. The five are not always described in exactly the same way, but they remain recognizable. For example, John Cassian, the great teacher of prayer in the fifth century, spoke of the fourfold nature of prayer. He based this on 1 Timothy 2:1, "First of all, then, I urge that supplications, prayers, intercessions, and thanksgivings be made." Cassian understands "supplication" to mean our expression of penitence and our asking for pardon. The Greek word here that "prayers" translates comes from the same root as the word for *vows*. So this part includes making our vows to God and corresponds to our fifth ingredient, dedication. Intercession and thanksgiving are the third and fourth ingredients we described, and the whole of this is set in the context of, and breathes the atmosphere we described as, adoration. All these ingredients are essential parts of the love experience and contribute to the content of the conversation between the believer and God. They enable us to be true to our created nature and to take our place in the order of redemption.

We do not pray merely because we like the feeling. Any person who prays regularly will tell you that prayer is not always emotionally rewarding. Some find it hardly ever is. We can pray for days, weeks, sometimes months, and even years, without getting any great emotional charge out of it. When our faith is strong, the absence of emotional rewards does not matter, and we continue to believe in God's presence even when we do not feel it. But sometimes our faith is weak and we doubt. This is when the will to pray is tested. If God rushed in and gave us a warm glow to keep us hooked, we would be addicts, not lovers. God is faithful, and if we continue to pray when our faith is weak, he will give us the gift of fidelity. Praying that lacks the rewards of warmth, or the confidence and assurance that come so easily when our faith is strong, is still valuable to us. Our prayer life grows stronger during those times that we mistake for dryness. We may often feel arid and lost in a desert; yet we are drawing on the divine well springs when we pray, whether or not we feel and know it. If we do not panic or despair when prayer seems dull and pointless, we shall learn to recognize that the benefits of prayer for the disciplined disciple in the doldrums, easily match what is gained by the more manic manifestations of some mystical experience.

In good times or bad we pray because we are in a relationship of love with God. This relationship needs to be nurtured by regular communication and enjoyment of the lover's presence. Lovers also want to get to know each other better. A very important reason for prayer is to get to know God better in order to become more perfectly united with him in love.

4   Getting to know God through contemplation

Once we have established the habit of committing five to ten minutes every day to prayer, we shall find some days when that brief period is too short. Ten minutes may not be long enough. In our short time of prayer each day we have tried to be consciously in God's presence, and in conversation with him we have shared our deepest feelings and concerns. As we have listened to the promptings of the Holy Spirit within us, we have gained insights into God's ways and his nature. We are now getting to know him, and we want to take more time to get to know him better. This is the stage at which we ought to decide to take an additional ten to thirty minutes for what we call contemplation or meditation. You may not be able to do this every day. Once or twice a week can be very helpful. Admittedly, it is easier to learn the few simple methods needed if we practise frequently, but it is discouraging to promise ourselves that we shall do something daily and then find that we fail to do so. It is better to make a realistic commitment of time and then increase it later if you find that possible.

The additional time we give to prayer is devoted to becoming better acquainted with God and his ways. It is tempting to think that because ten minutes of adoration, penitence, petition, thanksgiving, and dedication were good, then twenty minutes will be twice as good, and thirty minutes a threefold improvement. Yet, rather than merely doing more of the same, we ought to add something different. We need to continue with the regular disciplined short time of balanced prayer and then add a special time for contemplation or meditation. These two different styles of prayer, contemplation and meditation, both focus on deepening our experience of God.

Defining contemplation and meditation can be confusing because the terminology is not used consistently by all who follow these two roads to a deeper knowledge of God. For example, when non-Christian eastern religions speak of meditation, they describe something that sounds very similar to what we shall call contemplation. Whatever we call them, the two ways themselves are not difficult to distinguish. *Contemplation* seems very still and passive. Silence is prized, words are shunned, and the aim is to achieve utter simplicity in the direct experience of God. *Meditation*, on the other hand, is more obviously active. Words, pictures, the imagination, and the intellect, are welcomed and used as aids through which God communicates with us.

According to some theories of prayer we progress from the stage of vocal prayer in which we repeat the prayers we have learned and use words to speak to God, through the stage of mental prayer in which we use the methods of meditation, until we graduate to contemplation and the prayer of silence. I am in no position to challenge that as one good way to follow. However, it is clear that many people take more naturally to contemplation than to meditation, and they would be wasting their efforts by taking an uncongenial detour to a road they could have been travelling from the beginning. Others enjoy a rich experience with meditation and find contemplation too far removed from the way their mind seems to work. Personally I have only travelled the first steps of either way and believe that it is possible to enjoy both — although if you have only fifteen minutes available, you will obviously need to choose one or other approach for that time. Both ways are easy to begin. Having started along them, progress depends entirely on your willingness to continue.

Contemplation is very simple. Because it is so simple, it appears easy to teach. But since it requires a lot of practice, it is thought to be difficult to learn. Like riding a bicycle, theory is of little importance, and completely useless without practice. Contemplation is not difficult in itself, but it requires discipline and perseverance. In contemplation we simply seek and experience the presence of God. We do not want to tell him anything, and we are not looking for any messages from him. The focus is on God himself. This is like the silence in a good love relationship; it is enough simply to be together. Now, if you find that you can already relax, shut out distractions, concentrate your mind, and know yourself to be in contact with God, then you do not need to learn a method to get into that state. The method is merely a way to get there. No method is needed when you have arrived, for you are with God, and all that you could possibly desire is to be with him. The method to get there is called the psycho-technical method (*A Study of Gregory Palamas*, John Meyendorff, Faith Press, p. 25). In it we use psychological or psychosomatic techniques to alter our state of consciousness.

One form of this method is the use of the Prayer of Jesus. The words of the Jesus Prayer are, "Lord Jesus Christ, Son of God, have mercy on me." The prayer is used by a continual repetition of these words. We simply use them over and over again. The prayer may be lengthened by the addition of "a sinner" at the end. It is frequently shortened by the omission of "Son of God" or the final phrase. It can be reduced to "Lord have mercy" or even to one word, "Jesus" or "Lord." Although one word is enough, it is better to start with "Lord Jesus Christ, Son of God, have mercy on me," and adjust your practice later. To many modern Western minds the repetitiveness of this prayer seems foolish. The only way to discover what it is like is to try it.

The aim of the continual repetition is to allow the prayer to escape from our lips and our minds, and become the prayer of the heart. When we first use it, we shall be thinking of the meaning of the words. Once we are satisfied that they are good words, we can stop thinking about them and let go with our minds. In one way this is a skill that we acquire through practice, like learning to read silently without forming the words out loud. Just as we no longer need to say words with our lips in order for them to be in our minds, so we can go a further step and relax our intellectual activity and allow the words to enter our hearts. We can have words on our lips without thinking about their meaning, and we can have words full of meaning in our thoughts without them touching the heart of our being. The Jesus Prayer passes through the superficial levels of lips and minds, and operates in the heart. If you prefer to think of the heart as a blood pump, then what we are really talking about is the centre or core of our being, a profound level of consciousness far removed from active thoughts.

The words of the Jesus Prayer are to be trusted. They have been used for centuries. They cannot hurt us at the centre of self. What they can do is help our self to enter the company of the other Self who is God, and then to move into communion and union with him. In summary, having decided that we want to add about twenty minutes to our quiet time of prayer, we simply take that time to repeat the words of the Jesus Prayer. In doing this we shall get to know God more intimately and experience his presence more deeply.

Those who developed and preserved the tradition

of the Prayer of Jesus usually added one or two other techniques to the method. One was controlled breathing. To do this you breathe slowly and deeply while repeating the Jesus Prayer in rhythm with your breathing. You may say it once or twice each time you inhale and exhale. The frequency does not matter but the regularity does. Once the rhythm and the slowness and stillness have asserted themselves, you do not need to think of either the words or the breathing. An additional practice, which sounds exotic to us, caused amusement to some sophisticated critics of the Eastern monks who used this prayer in the thirteenth and fourteenth centuries. This was their fixing of the eyes on the middle of the body. These monks, whom we call hesychasts — from *hesychia*, meaning stillness, rest, quiet — were ridiculed as *omphalopsychoi* (i.e. their souls were in their navels). Some modern devotees of yoga have similarly been nicknamed navel-gazers. Obviously this fixing of the eyes is a technique to aid concentration and is meaningless by itself. Once you close your eyes for this kind of prayer, your mind's eye wants to see as little as possible and to remain motionless. Be still.

The spiritual tradition that developed this method was seeking for a way to "pray without ceasing" as Saint Paul exhorted the Thessalonians (1 Thessalonians 5:17). So this was not intended as a simple psycho-physical technique for beginners who want to pray in short periods of silent contemplation. Nevertheless it works for beginners. Therefore it is not a misappropriation of this technique if we use it for a few minutes a day. As a matter of fact, the few minutes we devote to contemplation will be enriched if we use the Jesus Prayer at other times also. I am definitely not recommending that you imitate the Russian writer of *The Way of a Pilgrim* (translated from the Russian by R.M. French, SPCK) who increased his capacity for repeating the prayer from three thousand times a day through six thousand to twelve thousand times daily over a period of less than two weeks. In a much less obsessive way we can start to repeat it wherever we are and whatever we are doing. This helps to prepare us for our time of contemplation and also leads us toward what the hesychasts were seeking, a life of constant prayer.

Some people find that the Jesus Prayer does not seem to suit their needs. They may, however, benefit from using the same technique with different words or even with a single word. When John Cassian taught about prayer at the beginning of the fifth century, he advocated this same form of spiritual contemplation. From the Abbot Isaac he had learned that the words, "O God, make speed to save me: O Lord make haste to help me," had been used in the East by monks who pondered them and ceaselessly revolved them in their hearts (*The Conferences of John Cassian X*, Second Conference of Abbot Isaac, 10. *Nicene*

and Post-Nicene Fathers, vol. XI, Eerdmans p. 405).
The crucial part of the method is the restriction of the
mind to one verse or even one word. This is a form of
spiritual poverty or extreme simplicity. When we
trust ourselves to one simple phrase or a single word
we abandon control of our thoughts. As we repeat the
word over and over, we prevent our minds from
reasserting our self-possessed and independent ways
of thinking. Instead we become wide open to posses-
sion by the divine Spirit. We are available to God and
dependent upon him. Even when we find this difficult, we do not lose but gain from this method.
When we discover that our minds can have difficulty
with something as simple as praying one word, then
we shall stop trying to reach God by being clever or
good, and let him reach us, because we finally know
that we are totally dependent upon his love and grace.

The Guild of Health has found that silent prayer
meets a special need in today's world. They teach a
method of silent meditation which is a descendent of
the ancient tradition of contemplation. They advo-
cate the use of a single sentence and suggest many
suitable verses of scripture. For example, you might
choose, "Lo, I am with you always" (Matthew
22:20), or "My peace I give unto you" (John 14:27), or
any similar verse that appeals to you. Having chosen
the words, you relax your body, remember the
presence of God, think briefly about the meaning of
the words, and then relax the mind, stop thinking,

and silently, slowly, and continuously repeat the words. Finally, at the end of the allotted time, you say thank you to God. If other thoughts pop into our minds — and they will — we do not worry but recall our chosen verse and resume our repetition of it.

This method has obvious similarities to the use of a mantra in Eastern religions. Yet it can be used with confidence by Christians because it is an ancient and well tried part of our own tradition. Our aim is knowledge of God the Holy Trinity. Our partner in the silent conversation is God himself. Furthermore, the words that we use to achieve the silence, and that we allow into our hearts, have orthodox Christian meaning, even though we are not consciously directing our attention to that meaning but focussing on the person and presence of our divine companion in prayer.

Although the idea of contemplation is extremely simple, we appear to have difficulty with it. We refuse silence and resist stillness. Instead of accepting moments of tranquillity, we disturb them by some effort or activity. The regular use of the psycho-technical method will help us to relax our resistance to silence and receive it as a grace from God.

Do not be discouraged if your mind keeps active when you want it to be still. Our culture and conditioning contribute to this busy way of behaving. Contemplation counters this and allows our basic humanity to rediscover the value of being still in the love of God. We are not always outwardly aware of this inner quietness when we practice the prayer of the heart. A faithful discipline will help us to persevere even when we cannot see any progress. Sometimes, thank God, we are surprised by silence and have to admit to ourselves with some amazement that we have truly felt the divine presence. I hope that I am not merely trying to excuse my failure to climb the spiritual heights when I suggest that it does not really matter if this very wonderful feeling is not frequently experienced. I believe that the real value of the experience is in being with God, and in allowing time for him in contemplation, whether or not we feel it is "working."

The benefits are often more easily detected in the state of our mind and spirit for the rest of the day than in the twenty minutes during which we repeated our prayer of the heart. We may discover that we feel relaxed and refreshed even after a quiet time when it was a particularly difficult struggle to concentrate. We may look for the wrong things and therefore mistakenly think that we have not experienced stillness and silence. We ought not to expect a fanfare of angelic trumpets to alert us to our inner quietness. The prayer of silence is marked by simplicity, not dramatic effects. Jesus taught that the kingdom of heaven is for the poor in spirit. This method is for those who know their need for God. Jesus promised that they would be blessed.

5 Getting to know God through meditation

In the time we devote to establishing a more intimate relationship with God, we may choose to follow the way of meditation. Unlike contemplation, which is the prayer of the heart, meditation makes use of the mind, the imagination, and the intellect, as well as the heart. I believe that we should all use meditation in addition to contemplation, but not necessarily as frequently. Meditation does not need to be formal. Like contemplation, meditation in an informal, spontaneous, or unplanned way can become a habit that pervades and enriches our daily living. Before this happens we shall probably need to discipline ourselves to follow a formal method of meditation for an allocated time, according to a regular plan. I shall suggest one well tried approach based on the method taught by Saint Ignatius Loyola in the sixteenth century. You will need to develop your own variations on the method or to choose an alternative. The method itself is merely a way to put yourself into a position where you are open to God's revelation of himself. God wants to communicate with us. All we need to do is learn to listen.

A formal meditation can be divided into four parts. The first part is preparation, which includes choosing the subject of the meditation and deciding when and where to do it. It will also include the opening or preparatory prayer of the meditation time. The second part is getting a clear picture or idea in our mind. The third part is to consider this idea from different angles and to examine it as closely as our concentration will allow. The fourth part is when we talk to God about the picture or thought in our mind and try to hear what he is saying to us.

In practice the meditation might follow a very simple program. On Sunday morning at the Eucharist you might decide that this week you are definitely going to spend twenty minutes in meditation. On Sunday afternoon you decide that although the coming week looks hectic, you can be sure of getting to bed early on Thursday. So you promise yourself that you will get up half an hour earlier than usual on Friday and commit ten minutes for your regular prayers and twenty minutes for meditation early that morning. You will waste most of the twenty minutes unless you decide in advance what the subject matter of the meditation will be. A list of suitable subjects would be endless, and it is better to make a random choice than to let the range paralyse our ability to choose. Stories from the Gospels are particularly good material for meditation.

You may decide that something from the crucifixion story would be appropriate for meditation on a Friday. So, on Sunday afternoon, you take a quick glance over the story of the Passion in chapter twenty-three of Saint Luke's Gospel. As you read, perhaps verse thirty-four stands out: ''And Jesus said, Father forgive them; for they know not what they do. And they cast lots to divide his garments.'' If this is what grabs your attention, then pick this verse and scene for your meditation. Between Sunday and Thursday you will occasionally think of the verse as you go about other activities. On Thursday, in your final evening prayers, include a rereading of at least verse thirty-four and, if possible, the whole of chapter twenty-three from Luke's Gospel. This will refresh your memory and allow the passage to be somewhere in your mind as you sleep. When you wake on Friday morning, try to turn your first thoughts to God, and recall the verse. After you have got organized and finished your regular ten minutes of prayer, if you plan to do it then, you are ready to begin the twenty minutes of meditation. Obviously the particular times, days, and subject matter can be varied. An excellent variation is to plan to visit a convenient Church building and spend twenty minutes in meditation there on your way home from work. All of the preceding is advance preparation.

The final stage of preparation is what we do at the beginning of the twenty minutes of meditation. First, we may make the sign of the cross in the name of the Father, and of the Son, and of the Holy Spirit, recalling that we are in God's presence and at his disposal. If our meditation is following immediately after our regular prayer time, there is no need to repeat our confession. Otherwise this immediate preparation ought to include a brief expression of penitence and an acknowledgement that we are unworthy. After this we use an invocation of the Holy Spirit. The best known is the Veni Creator (p. 109). Some people find it very helpful in the next three stages of the meditation to have before them a clean sheet of paper with the text for meditation written at the top. In each of the remaining stages one jots down points to be recalled.

The second stage in the meditation is to picture the scene, trying to hear the words in their original life context. Without going too far back in the story, we may wish to review the events that led to this point where Jesus is actually being nailed to the cross. Try to hear the sounds, to see the soldiers, the criminals, and the onlookers, and to imagine that you are one of those present. Feel the temperature, and smell the mixture of the familiar and the frightening in the air. Then try to hear Jesus saying, "Father, forgive . . ." as you see and hear the nails being driven. And watch the soldiers finish their business and move on to gamble for Jesus's few remaining possessions.

This second stage of imagination (traditionally called "representation" and perhaps best described as "imaging") flows imperceptibly into the third stage of consideration. You now try to think of each point separately and revolve it in your mind. Ponder. What levels of meaning are there? For example, who is being forgiven: the soldiers only, or all those who had a hand in bringing about his condemnation also; only those who sin in ignorance, or all sinners including yourself? What kind of attitude is required to speak such words? What kind of attitude ignores them and carries on to cast lots? The possibilities in this, as in all Gospel stories, are enormous. You will have to be prepared to cut yourself short at this stage if you are going to become engaged at the deeper level of talking to God about the subject of the meditation and your thoughts.

In the fourth stage of meditation we engage in what is called a colloquy. While we are deeply involved in the scene from the Gospel, and as we try to grasp what is happening, some things will puzzle us and others will impress us with new insights. We may have jotted down a word or two on our paper so that we do not lose track of these thoughts and questions. In this stage of colloquy we construct a conversation with God about what has happened so far in our meditation. We tell God how we feel about this scene. We ask him to help us to understand what has bewildered us. We ask if our new insight is what he meant us to see — and so on. Then we imagine his answers. The dialogue may continue for as long as we have the time available. If we have followed the first three steps, we shall not find it hard to imagine what God would answer to what we say in stage four. The exciting thing is that we often find that we have imagined a totally surprising answer. He says something in the conversation which we would not have expected to hear. Of course, at one level our minds are creating both sides of the conversation; but at a deeper level the divine Spirit will guide our thoughts, and some of what we shall hear is not really our creation at all but the revelation of God. We need to be careful about this. If we take ourselves too seriously, we may think we have developed an exclusive open line to God. But if we retain our sense of humour, we shall not become unbalanced as we find God entering this game of the imagination and lightly opening our minds to new ways of knowing him better.

In *The Spiritual Exercises* Saint Ignatius writes, "The colloquy is made, properly speaking, as a friend speaks to a friend, or a servant to his master, asking at one time for some grace, at another accusing oneself of some evil committed, at another making known one's affairs, and seeking counsel concerning them. And then to say Our Father." Not all meditations lead into an extended imaginary conversation with God. Sometimes we are left with no more than a simple petition which we address to God, confident that he put it into our heart and will hear it. In this stage of meditation it is particularly helpful to jot down brief notes to remind ourselves afterwards of some of the fruits of our meditation. The time will pass quickly, and the Lord's Prayer is a good conclusion.

This basic four part method of meditation allows many variations. The subject matter need not be restricted to the Gospels, although the Bible and the central themes of the Christian tradition ought to be the predominant sources of our meditation material. We described stage two as an imaginative representation of the story of a historical event. Even if the subject matter is a myth, a poem, an aphorism, or a very abstract idea, we still need stage two before stage three. The aim is to turn the imagination loose and give it the freedom to range widely, to involve us in the subject, to let us see with fresh eyes and hear with wide open ears, before we allow our critical faculties to become actively employed in stage three. Although the third stage of consideration tries to avoid the trap of merely linear logic, it will inevitably restrain some of our wilder or more daring imaginings. Some subjects allow more scope for the active and creative imagination, while others more readily engage the intellect in following logical implications and attempting to integrate complex insights. At times our emotions are deeply involved; on other occasions our wills are stirred up to resolution and commitment. Always by the time we participate in the colloquy we have moved to a deeper level where the centre of our being is in communion with God. Christian meditation cannot remain an imaginative, intellectual, emotional, or volitional exercise. It is a spiritual exercise leading into personal communion with the living God. The intensity of this experience ought not to discourage experimentation.

The colloquy permits a wide variety of approaches. We may imagine a conversation with any of the three persons of the Trinity; or we can talk to the Blessed Virgin Mary, or one of the saints, or a bystander in the scene of our meditation; or we can construct a conversation with ourselves. The aim in every case is to be attentive to what God wants to reveal of himself. As in all forms of prayer the real conversation is with God. Because we are fragile, God deals with us gently. He rarely threatens or overwhelms us in meditation. He speaks quietly and uses a lot of indirect approaches. At some times in our lives we feel as if God has torpedoed our ship and then thrown us a life belt. We have to choose his salvation or perish. My guess is that most people experience meditation more like a boat gently coming alongside of us, and a hand is stretched out, and we are invited to leave our boat and step into his, and we sail together.

If you wish to use this method daily, it will wear very well. The duration can easily be extended beyond the span of twenty minutes. The method combines well with a prayer journal in which you record your thoughts for future use. In it you will preserve some treasures that would otherwise be lost.

It must be admitted that some people will never get around to the regular use of a method that requires so much discipline. An unstructured method may appeal to those who are afraid of being too rigid. We can be as flexible as we wish, and use any opportunity that comes, for informal meditation. Any time given to thinking about God with God is well spent, and we get to know God better whenever we spend a few minutes thinking with him. Most of us meditate in an informal way even when we do not give the activity that name. Slowly reading passages from the Bible and reflecting on their meaning is meditation. Steeping yourself in spiritual classics such as the writings of Julian of Norwich, Saint Teresa of Avila, Saint John of the Cross, or even non-Christian works like the Meditations of Marcus Aurelius, can also be a way of meditation. All that is necessary is to pick something worth the attention and then read it very slowly, revolving the thoughts in your mind. This is the opposite of speed reading, and the enemy is haste. Relax, do not rush, and be receptive. Jot down quotations you want to keep, and record those of your own thoughts to which you wish to return. (You may find it easier to complete your journal outside your meditation time.)

Even sanctified day dreaming could count as a form of meditation. Without reading a book or following a formal structure we can still ponder with God. Any thinking deliberately open to God is related to meditation.

If you discover that you enjoy meditation, you may be tempted to forget about contemplation altogether. Eventually you may decide quite correctly that one or other way is better for you. But I believe that we should keep our options open as beginners. I would regret having written anything about meditation if it distracted someone from following the way of silence. I believe we can follow both ways.

6   Aids to prayer

Aids and advice in abundance

An armchair mountaineer was so excited by a television program about the ascent of Everest that he was moved to drive to a sporting goods store to equip himself for climbing. There his enthusiasm was matched by that of an expert salesman. He acquired so many aids to mountaineering that he could scarcely stagger back to his car under the weight of his purchases. His armchair welcomed his return, and his closet now contains a mountain of books and equipment. There are a vast number of easily accessible aids to prayer and volumes of advice available — so be selective.

Time

"I don't have the time." We have all made this excuse to ourselves. An enormous aid to prayer would be the miraculous provision of the time to do it. Of course we cannot make time; so we must take the time. There are 1,440 minutes available to us every day we live. If you devote ten minutes to your regular prayer time, and use two minutes for a morning prayer and another two minutes at night, you will have almost reached a one per cent prayer level. This is a long way from prayer without ceasing. The proportions and the quantity are no measure of the quality and value of prayer, but it is salutary to realize how much more time we could use if we wished. Either we plan our own time, or circumstances beyond our control consume our days for us.

Because the kind of prayer we are discussing in this book appears to be a private activity, we sometimes feel that we are selfishly taking time for ourselves when we pray. This is nonsense. If we remember what Jesus said to Martha about Mary, and acknowledge that prayer is time with God and not solitary self-indulgence, then we know that we not only have the right to take this time; it is also our duty to do so. Even when we take into account the time devoted to all other religious activities as well as prayer, we still have ample time left to fulfil our obligations to others. We shall also be more loving and less selfish in our relationships with others because of the time we take for prayer.

Unless you plan a disciplined allocation of time for prayer, it will almost certainly be squeezed out of your life. Yet, because our life styles are so varied, it is impossible to be dogmatic about the best time to pray. Early morning suits me well, but if I were a single parent with young children, it might be the worst possible time. Each of us must pick the time we are most likely to be able to protect, then be resolute in our determination to take that time; and if something unavoidable invades that time, we must be equally determined to substitute some other time.

Place

It is easier to pray in a place where we can be quiet and undisturbed. If you live alone, then it is relatively easy to find a private place. In crowded accommodations it is much more difficult. The minimum aim is a place where we can at least be still and not have to get up or move about. A quiet room with a crucifix or icon is ideal. If you feel frustrated or deprived of quiet at home, then it is probably a good idea to plan to visit a church building from time to time. There you may find a congenial environment conducive to prayer. Enjoy an extended quiet time there, and then do the best you can on a daily basis at home without resenting or worrying about the distractions you cannot avoid.

Visiting a church building for personal prayer at times other than the hours of public worship can be a tremendous aid to all of us. There is no such thing as an ''empty'' church building any more than there can strictly speaking be ''private'' prayer. We are always in the divine presence, and we are inseparable from the community of the Church. Most churches are open during daylight hours, and in them you can discover an oasis of tranquillity where you breathe the atmosphere of spirituality. If your church has the custom of reserving the Blessed Sacrament, this will be an additional aid to devotion. Simply kneel or stand before the tabernacle or aumbry, pray without words, or slowly recite the Anima Christi (p. 110). In our century we have become so afraid that we might seem to be putting God in a box that we have become embarrassed by the notion of sacred space. Since God's presence is everywhere, we can pray anywhere. But we have not slipped into superstition when we find that a quiet sanctuary allows us to escape from many distractions and helps us to focus our attention on the spiritual dimension of life.

Posture

For most people in most homes the best posture is probably sitting in a comfortable but upright chair. Lying down is too relaxing, unless you are an invalid confined to bed. Kneeling seems to be easier in churches than in most homes. Walking suits some styles of prayer, but it is not always conducive to inner stillness. However, if we are feeling restless and have a particular subject in mind, then going for a walk with God and holding an imagined conversation on the way can work very well. Standing is an excellent position for some kinds of prayer and works particularly well before an icon, crucifix, or statue. Your hands can be lifted up, stretched out, held open, folded, or forgotten. I find the lotus position too uncomfortable to be useful, and I could not get into it now if I wanted too! I went through a stage of praying while standing on my head. This was a useful change of perspective, but my head became sore. In prayer it is important to take neither your posture nor your person too seriously.

The only way to discover which postures are best for you is to experiment with them, bearing in mind that an erect spine seems to be a key factor. Your aim is to put your body into a position in which you can forget it. You want to be relaxed yet alert, still, silent, and receptive. Slow breathing is an aid, provided that we do not allow the process to distract us from the prayer. If you cannot decide which is the best position to try first, sit in a comfortable upright chair, put both of your feet flat on the floor, keep your spine reasonably straight, rest your hands on your legs in a comfortable position above your knees, close your eyes, exhale completely, then breathe naturally, and you are ready to start. You will obviously have to adjust a little to remain comfortable, open your eyes if you want to read, and move your hands if you want to hold a book or make a note. Such movements are not distractions. After all you are not attempting to imitate a statue; you are trying to be at ease in God's company.

Prayers composed by others

Prayer includes words and silence. The silence is more precious than the words. In silence the Word is made known to us; our silence is our openness to God's self-revelation. Words, however, are also essential in prayer, even if they do not have the scarcity value of silence. In conversation with God it is good to use our own words, speaking freely; we do not need to rely on a script. Nevertheless "pre-packaged" prayers composed by others can help us greatly. I could not have continued to pray over the years without a heavy reliance on other people's words. Almost everything I have ever wanted to say to God has been expressed by someone else better than I could articulate it. Similarly, when I have believed that I was hearing what God had to say, it has almost always been in words from the Bible, or the Prayer Book, from some spiritual or secular writing, or in something I heard from another's lips. Set forms of prayer are among the benefits we receive from the Christian community. They are gifts we can share with each other and through which the community supports its members, even when we appear to be praying alone. In fact they are our own words, and we own them because they belong to our community.

There are thousands of prayers available in print. The Bible is the greatest of all printed resources for prayer. Everyone should use not only the Lord's Prayer and the Psalms but also selections from the other prayers of scripture. It is even easier to find usable forms in the *Book of Common Prayer*. A hymn book provides a wide choice of words for many different kinds of prayer. You will find that a few of the hymns make truly superb private prayers when repeated slowly and thoughtfully. There are many anthologies of prayer on sale. Browse through some of them and get advice on which are worthwhile from your priest or a friend. In most religious book stores you will find a shelf or two stocked with the classics of spirituality. They provide grist for the mill in your prayers and guidance for your spiritual life. Please do not try to read all of the mystics immediately. They take a lot of digesting and are best read slowly and thoughtfully. It is tempting to assemble a library of printed resources and become a student of prayer. This is not the same as praying. You can escape from the bookshelf by making your own collection of prayers in a looseleaf notebook. A few of the classics of prayer are included in the appendix.

When prayer is difficult, no matter how worried,

depressed, or exhausted we may feel, we can still repeat the Lord's Prayer or another set form. We may even have difficulty believing what we say; but we are praying. It is impossible for this not to "work." There is no such thing as failure in prayer. Because prayer is God's will and he reaches out to us, he will always be in communication with us when we pray. Consciously we may be in too much of a mess to be aware of his reality and presence, yet he remains faithful. God is completely reliable. When we are in "the depths," any form of prayer will do for us to open ourselves to God. Obviously, if we are able to be selective, then some forms will help us more than others. The fact that any prayer will do when we are desperate, provides a clue to why it is that words are not strictly needed at all. The core of prayer is communion with God. Communion with God is his purpose for us in creation and redemption. All that we need to do is turn to him. But when we are in the depths, a set form is a reassuring lifebelt. Persistent prayer at what look like the low points in our spiritual life can lead to amazing progress. Using a set form is like flying on automatic pilot; we may not be up to directing or enjoying the prayer, yet we continue to "say our prayers" by repeating words, and discover that we are flying.

Thank God we have high points as well as low points in our spiritual journey. When we are spiritually alert, the use of the same words will feel quite different from when we repeated them in desperation. Words that we have recited hundreds of times before will explode with new meaning, and fresh insights will flash from familiar phrases. The basic explanation for this is that God is revealing himself to us in the prayer. From one perspective the words are merely poor human vehicles which can never be adequate to express the mystery beyond them. From the human point of view, however, the words of classic prayers are among the finest words that humanity has achieved. They are rich with the associations and meanings of the centuries. The intensity and sincerity with which they have been prayed have been assimilated to them. The insights of millions are not immediately retrievable by an individual person, but they enrich the community's understanding and wisdom, some of which is accessible to us at any given time. In spite of their symbolic denseness and rich complexity of meanings, the words of prayers such as the Lord's Prayer or the Anima Christi are extremely simple and transparent to the reality they express. No one needs to feel clever in order to use them.

Memorize some of the classic prayers to use whenever the opportunity arises during the day. Persevere in their use when you think you are too busy to pray, and keep repeating them even when your faith is so fragile that you wonder whether it is worth praying at all. We ought never to despise or neglect traditional forms of prayer. No one that I know lives in the silence of mystical prayer all of the time, or even much of the time. We all need good words to keep us within the prayer of the community and to avoid individualistic, idiosyncratic, and elitist piety.

Arrow prayers

Arrow prayers are short prayers which we store in the quiver of our memory to shoot off to God whenever we think of doing so. They work well when we are very busy or under stress. Because an arrow prayer is very short, it can be used while we are occupied with any activity. Lines from the liturgy make good arrows. Before we speak we may say silently, "O Lord open thou my lips." When we begin a difficult task we can let "Lord make haste to help us" flash through our mind. The Jesus Prayer can be used as an arrow prayer. As soon as we realize that we have done something we regret or have fallen short of our aim to love as God loves, we can pray, "God forgive me." When something good happens we think, "Thank God." Collect and make your own short prayers. They help to sanctify our daily lives and to move toward prayer without ceasing.

Art and beauty

Poetry, music, the visual arts, and natural beauty can all help us to pray. In choosing aids to enrich and enhance our prayer life, we need not restrict ourselves to art forms classified as religious; although we shall not feel deprived if we do so, for some of humanity's greatest achievements are in religious art, literature, and music. Some of this art is created in order to aid prayer. The holy icons of Eastern Christianity are painted according to strict religious rules by artists after arduous and intense spiritual preparation, so that the icon itself will be a meeting between heaven and earth. Many other paintings are clearly intended to be devotional aids. Even when we are less sure of the artist's purpose, a work of art can stimulate prayer.

There are two main approaches to the use of art and natural beauty in prayer. The first and more obvious way is to confront the poem, symphony, painting, mountain, flower, and to concentrate on it, trying to share the mystery beyond it, toward which it points. This can often yield very rewarding results. At times we shall be moved, uplifted, enlightened, or even experience ecstasy. (Ecstasy is standing outside of oneself, and art and beauty are among the safest ways of being taken out of ourselves.)

The other way is to share an aesthetic experience with God. Put on a record or go to a concert, and say

to yourself, "I am going to listen to this with God."
Then give yourself to the music, but remain aware
that you are in God's presence. Whether you go to the
ballet, visit an art gallery, or climb a mountain, a
beautiful experience shared with God is a way of
prayer. Just as human lovers enrich and enhance their
relationship by common experience, so our union
with God is nurtured when we who share his love of
beauty, consciously appreciate it with him.

Organized quiet times and retreats

Many dioceses, monasteries, convents, and parishes
organize quiet days and retreats to foster the growth
of spiritual life. Your parish priest will be able to tell
you what is available in your area. These events take
many forms and usually include corporate worship,
guided meditation, the opportunity for individual
counselling as well as a lot of silence and the ideal environment to pray without distractions. Retreats are
sometimes feared by those who have not experienced
them. Actually it is easier to relax into a weekend
retreat than to keep quiet for only half a day. The
slower pace of the longer period is better for beginners. It may seem a luxury to take two or three days
and nights for a residential retreat, yet as the frenzy of
modern life intensifies, retreats may become neces-
sities not only for our spiritual well-being but even

for our sanity. A weekend in a religious house or retreat centre, with no external demands, with all our physical needs well cared for, with no need even to speak, allows us to be comfortable, relaxed, and open. It is well worth indulging in this joy once a year. A well conducted retreat helps us to become more proficient in prayer and therefore has lasting benefits in our spiritual lives.

Help from the praying community

There is an intimate connection between corporate prayer and the individual's personal prayer. Our own secret or internal prayer is enabled, encouraged, and nourished by the praying community. There is secular scientific evidence that many apparently individual activities become easier to accomplish as increasing numbers of other people do them. When some animals are taught new skills, the first to learn take much longer to reach proficiency than those at a later stage, after a critical mass of the population has adopted the new behaviour. If only one person in the world were to pray, it would be heroic and wellnigh impossible. In a society where very few pray, it is difficult. In a community where all are praying, we are not only encouraged by each others' examples; we are also enabled by the change in our collective consciousness, which makes prayer as natural as breathing. Even when we are physically alone and not consciously aware of any other Christian praying, at a deeper level we remain united by the Spirit and support each other in prayer.

A spiritual guide

If the novice mountaineer at the beginning of this chapter should ever set foot on a mountain, I hope he takes a guide as well as his gear. A personal guide is a great aid to prayer. We may choose a spiritual friend with whom we feel free to talk about our experience of prayer. Or we may wish to go to an acknowledged practitioner as our spiritual director. We may use our confessor to advise us on prayer. We may be satisfied by occasionally checking out our progress and discussing our problems informally with our pastor. Some people find that their current "guru" is a book in which they are absorbed, which is influencing them, and which they are using for guidance. Some of us are more private persons than others, but all of us need to confide in someone else and get outside counsel at some time or other. No one needs to feel isolated in their spiritual journey.

All the help we need

Remember that there is always more help available to you than you can use. There is more excuse for being overwhelmed by the abundance than starved from the lack of aids to prayer. Yet many people experience intense spiritual loneliness. They believe that they are on their own with no resources and no help for them. Visit your parish church, your parish priest, a religious book store, or talk to a friend who you know is a praying Christian. You will discover that you are one of a vast throng of pilgrims on this way. Together we have all the help we need.

7   Prayers with a purpose

No prayers are without purpose, but some have highly focussed and particular purposes. For example, we may pray for guidance in making a decision or for healing from a particular infirmity. In this chapter we shall examine briefly some of the more common ways of praying with special intention.

Praying for guidance

All of us must make decisions. Some decisions are crucial for the future direction of our lives and our relationships. In these cases we may become very anxious. Afraid to make a mistake we pray to God for guidance. When we have embarked on the Christian journey, we are committed to obeying the will of God. This requires that we ask ourselves what God wills for us before we make a choice. The answer is not always obvious, so we turn to God in prayer. Abraham, Moses, the prophets, the Virgin Mary, the Apostles, and the saints of our tradition all reinforce our conviction that we ought to follow our vocation — the call of God. Yet how do we know what our vocation is? Traditionally we have been taught to pray for the inspiration of the Holy Spirit to guide our decision.

Sometimes this guidance comes easily. In our daily

prayers we may tell God that we are having difficulty in making a certain choice and need his help. To help articulate this need we could repeat slowly and thoughtfully the words of the hymn, "Breathe on me, breath of God" (*The Hymn Book*, no. 240), bearing in mind the choices open to us. As we pray it may become very obvious that certain actions would be totally inappropriate and that God is pointing us in one very particular direction. All that remains to do then is to thank God for his guidance and follow his will.

At other times we may need to put a lot more mental effort into the decision, over a period of many weeks. Perhaps we have repeatedly and sincerely asked for the guidance of the Holy Spirit without reaching any inner conviction of what God would have us do. We are totally bewildered. Now, prayer is not a substitute for reason and wise choices cannot be made by magic. Yet, assuming that we are using our wits and common sense to the full, we may still feel the need to pray. We may have written on paper a balance sheet of the pros and cons of a course of action. Weighed financially we get one answer; judged by personal preference there is a different result. We do not introduce God as a tie-breaker, but things can look quite different when we see them in God's presence. Will this advance his kingdom of love and justice? Will I become more like Christ if I do that? Measured by standards of holiness and righteousness, how do I rate the alternatives?

Remembering that in prayer God is with us and that prayer for guidance is not a solitary mental struggle, we try to relax enough, and trust enough, to be open to the promptings of the divine Spirit. This may point us in an entirely new direction that had not previously entered our mind or had earlier been too hastily dismissed. If we have very fixed ideas about something, it may take a long time in prayer before our minds are malleable under the will of God and receptive to the inspiration of the Holy Spirit. When God intends to reveal his will to us through prayer, we can be sure that, even if the invocation of the Holy Spirit and openness to his promptings do not work quickly, then perseverance will eventually lead to the illumination we seek. We shall reach a conviction that will allow us to act with confidence in a good conscience. Because we continue to be human, even when guided by the Holy Spirit, our moral confidence falls short of absolute certainty. In fact we need to do everything that we do admitting that we may be wrong. The alternative is insufferable arrogance.

In other situations it is clear that neither by scriptural revelation, nor by the Church's teaching, nor by guidance in prayer, does God intend to tell us what to do, other than use the divine freedom he shares with us. In straining for guidance we can create a problem for ourselves. When we sincerely desire to do God's will, we shall not ask him to reveal his purpose for us so that we can decide whether or not to do it, hoping to get the satisfaction of God's authorization for what we have already decided to do with or without his blessing. Let us assume that we are not playing that game and that we persevered and struggled honestly in prayer; yet his will remains hidden from us. At this stage we ought to ask ourselves if we are trying to make God too narrow and rigid.

Some people regard life as a mine field, arranged as a maze, with only one safe way out. God has a map of the hidden labyrinth, but on the surface we can only see ourselves in the middle of an open hayfield. One wrong step and we shall be blown to smithereens! Yet God perversely will not reveal more than one step at a time, and sometimes appears to be reluctant even to do that much. The scenario extracts from us the maximum of anxiety-ridden dependance, which, God forgive us, we mistake for faith. This, when stated so crudely, can be seen to be nonsense. Our theology of creation includes the insight that God creates far more potential than can ever be actualized. Whenever we choose, we inevitably leave undone many other potential actions, not because they were wrong, but because we are finite. In most of our choices what really matters is that we walk forward in love, faith, and hope, knowing that God is with us. If we genuinely and sincerely keep company with God in our prayers, we can confidently risk being wrong. God does not have a hidden agenda for every moment of our lives. We are given freedom, and we fulfil God's purpose in creation when we act as free moral agents and co-creators with him. In short, many choices are objectively indifferent, and the mines are in our imaginations, not the field. The field is open and safe when we walk with God.

Our prayer for guidance may lead us to relax and simply do what we believe is best at the time, fully aware that the choice is made by us. Perhaps this is the best kind of guidance because it springs from the confidence of being in a right relationship with God, rather than from the uncertainty of a stranger trying to guess the unpredictable workings of the mind of a dangerous and irritable tyrant. These comments are not meant to belittle the mental anguish that many experience in the search for guidance. In our Gethsemanes agony is unavoidable. We and many others live with the consequences of our choices which can be destructive and evil. The responsibility is awful. However, if we are open to God in prayer, the burden will not paralyse us. The prayer for guidance will be a very particular focus in our prayers from time to time, but obviously we do not turn to God for guidance only when we are puzzled. Our daily prayers will encourage us to try to live in continual harmony with the divine will.

Prayer and death

There are many ways of praying related to death, dying, and the departed. The awareness of death ought to be present in our prayers. It does not need to be prominent, but it must not be avoided.

There are some intriguing similarities between praying and dying. When we die we have to give up control over our own lives; we can no longer determine our own direction, and we move into an unknown experience. Similarly when we pray, we enter into communion with God and must allow him to control the conversation and the experience; we hand over the direction of our lives to him, and our union with God in prayer is a territory as unknown as death. In order to pray we must let go of our lives and let God unite us with himself: this could equally well be a description of Christian death.

In our prayers we acknowledge that we must die although we do not know when. Our prayer will be that we shall be prepared at the hour of our death and therefore that we be ready now. One of the most commonly used prayers, the Ave Maria, concludes with, "pray for us sinners now, and at the hour of our death." If you use visual images in your meditation, you might try for a few minutes to imagine yourself looking at your own body in your coffin, or standing beside your own grave. I do not recommend that you do this frequently, and while you ought to do this only after consulting with your spiritual adviser, I would warn you against telling everyone else, lest they conclude that you are hopelessly morbid or crazy or both. This kind of meditation seems acceptable for a medieval Spaniard but strange in a twentieth century Canadian. Yet we are all equally mortal.

It sometimes seems that more people fear sudden death lest they be found without clean underwear than those who are concerned for a good conscience. Meditating on our death at a time when we are completely healthy gives a marvellously fresh perspective on life and helps us to maintain a proper balance in our values. Far more than this, however, it will encourage us to pray Jesus's dying prayer, "Father, into thy hands I commit my spirit" (Luke 23:46). This act of faith and commitment is at the heart of all prayer, and when we do it, we have no further fear of death. When Saint Paul wrote, "I die daily" (1 Corinthians 15:31), he was referring to a spiritual, not a physical, activity. In doing this we enter into union with God and already share his eternal life.

Dealing with our own death is only part of handling our mortality. We also have to be with others as they die and to face the pain of bereavement. Dying is clearly helped by prayer. People who have never in their lifetime admitted the need to pray will welcome prayers on their death bed. There can be few more memorable and moving experiences than to be present at a death and say or hear the magnificent commendatory prayer:

> Depart, O Christian soul, out of this world,
> In the Name of God the Father Almighty, who created thee;
> In the Name of Jesus Christ, who redeemed thee;
> In the Name of the Holy Spirit, who sanctifieth thee.
> May thy rest be this day in peace, and thy dwelling-place in the Paradise of God.
> (*Book of Common Prayer*, 1959 Canada, p. 590)

What more can we say? The dying have a place in our prayers.

We also pray for the departed, publicly in the liturgy of the community, and privately in our personal prayers. In bereavement prayer for a departed loved one is a great comfort. Even though we know next to nothing about what it is like to have died, we believe that the faithful departed are with God and in his presence at least as intimately as we are in prayer. In communion with God we are in communion with all other persons who share that communion, whether they are living on earth or have already died. Even when we are not feeling any particular bereavement, it is appropriate to include some thankful remembrance of the departed in our prayer. Prayer is conversation, and it would be a strange conversation which eliminated all references to people as soon as they died or after we recovered from the grief of their loss.

Prayer and sickness

Prayer in sickness and intercessions for the sick are among the most common manifestations of contemporary prayer. An adequate discussion of this phenomenon would need to be set in the context of the Church's ministry of healing, which is beyond the scope of this brief book.

If our own sickness is involved, we shall naturally talk to God about our condition when we talk to him about everything else. If there is a lot of suffering involved, we are likely to be very insistent in asking for healing and courage. It may be that we recover, and then our prayers will include thanksgiving for this. Remember that neither prayers for healing nor thanksgiving for the restoration of health should take over the whole of our conversation with God. A sick person who talks about nothing but sickness is sicker than he thinks, and a healthy one who repeats the story of recovery like a broken record is not as well as he says. Furthermore, physical healing does not automatically follow a correctly recited formula of prayer. There is no magic. Saint Paul repeatedly prayed for his own healing but was not healed. The answer he received is far more help to us and apparently satisfied him. It was, "My grace is sufficient for you, for my power is made perfect in weakness" (2 Corinthians 12:9).

We also pray for others who are sick and suffering. Because our love for others is inseparable from our love for God, it is natural that our conversation with God will include our concerns for those in specific need. As with ourselves, so in our prayer for others, we accept that holding them up in God's presence is the heart of what we do. If we are in a right relationship with God, then at the deepest level we experience wholeness. Since health is related to wholeness, then through prayer we can at least expect healing of sickness caused by our spiritual malaise; and when miracles happen, thank God! For the rest we can be confident that we will receive spiritual strength to endure adversity. Much remains to be said beyond these minimal statements. For our purposes all we need to say is that we ought to pray for wholeness and healing when we are sick and for the healing of others. An intercession list of the names of those of our family, friends, and fellow parishioners who are ill, is a useful aid to memory. Even people who have not been physically healed will tell you how much they have appreciated the prayers of their fellow Christians, and will claim to have been assisted by them. Even though we do not understand how the process works, we ought to keep these persons in our prayers.

Prayer for protection

In ancient times prayer for protection was very common. Because we find it difficult to fear some of the things which frightened previous generations, we may not identify with many ancient prayers. Yet we all feel threatened at times, and when that sense becomes acute, it is important to acknowledge the threat and bring it into a prayer for protection. When we experience temptation, we ought to ask for divine assistance. Saint Patrick's Breastplate (*The Hymn Book*, no. 68) is far more than a petition for protection; but if we use it as a prayer, we shall feel the strength that comes from knowing that we are defended by the Holy Trinity.

Other intentions

There are many other particular purposes on which we focus in prayer. Important among these are the prayer of preparation for the sacrament of Holy Communion, the prayer of penance when we do a thorough self-examination and confession of sin, prayers to sanctify time, including morning, noonday, and evening prayers aimed at acknowledging the holiness of every hour, and the prayer of thanksgiving which may be related to a birth, a wedding, a reunion, or anything from the range of life's experiences which make us glad and grateful.

Prayer for union with God

Underlying all the particular purposes for prayer is a single purpose related to our basic human need. This is the need for God. We pray because we need God. In the secularized world we inhabit, we tend to live by an illusion that suffocates us. We live as if the material world were the whole of reality; and in this stifling materialistic world of our stunted imagination there is not enough air to fill our spiritual lungs. We need to escape from the illusion, discover the spiritual dimension of life, contact reality, and breathe deeply and freely the fresh air of the Spirit. That is what we do in prayer. When life is particularly difficult, prayer feels like opening a prison window and seeing sunlight and flowers, and smelling sweet air. We escape into the reality of God. When things are more as they ought to be, we shall not imagine ourselves looking out from a cell but walking freely with God into the fresh and open future. If we come to God in prayer, then he unites us with himself; this is our purpose and his intention.

8 Difficulties

Because prayer is ultimately simple and natural, I have been deliberately understating the difficulties. However, any person who has tried to pray for many years is unlikely to underestimate the seriousness of the difficulties and obstacles in the life of prayer. We cannot catalogue all the problems here, but we can mention a few and indicate some solutions.

The first difficulty with prayer is that it is too simple for us. In principle it is no more difficult for us to pray than to breathe. God creates us and redeems us, and his purpose is that we should live with him in a relationship of love and communion. If we think of prayer as a meeting, then it is God who proposes the tryst, and he will be present. All we need to do is make ourselves available. We can turn this simplicity into an obstacle by being either too proud or too humble.

If we are too proud, we shall scorn something that is accessible to all without any effort. We prefer to believe that prayer is very difficult and that communication with God can only be achieved by unwavering spiritual exertion. We may choose the way of fasting and self-denial, or the intellectual path of studying the methods of all the masters of prayer, or believe that it is our patience that will be rewarded. If our discovery that we truly meet God in prayer comes after a struggle, then we can be proud of our achievement, and reasonably sure that we are among an elite few who have scaled the spiritual heights. It is harder to appreciate something that any child can do.

On the other hand our problem may be mistaken humility. It is hard to accept that the creator of the universes should be concerned for one solitary human. Certainly this ought to amaze us, but not so much that we do not believe it. The gospel is that God loves each one of us and reaches out to all of us. If we can accept this with our heads, then we ought to be willing to let our hearts experience his love. As Saint Teresa told her sisters, "A fine humility it would be if I had the Emperor of Heaven and earth in my house, coming to it to do me a favour and to delight in my company, and I were so humble that I would not answer His questions, nor remain with Him, nor accept what He gave me, but left Him alone" (*The Way of Perfection*, trans. by E. Allison Peers, Image Books, p.184).

Faith is the solution to this first difficulty. We achieve union with God in prayer not by our efforts but by God's grace. All we need to do is trust him. Similarly, as our worthiness cannot achieve union, so our unworthiness cannot prevent it. God overcomes that obstacle also. If we think of merits, it should be of Christ's merits. He has bridged the gap between the divine perfection and the human condition. Will we be so ungrateful that we refuse to trust God to meet us in prayer, and will we reject him by leaving him alone? What we need first in prayer is not method or technique, but simple faith. Start praying, keep praying, and believe that no matter what happens or how you feel, God is with you, hears you, and unites himself with you at the deepest level of your being. And thank God that the success of the enterprise does not depend on you.

A second difficulty which many people identify is lack of concentration. When we pray our minds wander. If we are trying to follow a rigid method, then failures in concentration will be felt more acutely. In fact, they do not really matter much. Some people make a technique out of a wandering mind. They simply let the mind range where it will and bring whatever pops into their consciousness into their conversation with God. This is not a style that commends itself as our best effort in prayer; but it is a lot better than going into decline, or abandoning prayer, because we are not endowed with great gifts of concentration. (For people who concentrate easily the "stream of consciousness" approach would be a useful balance in their prayer to ensure that all parts of their lives are brought into their relationship with God, not only what they choose to concentrate on.) Some of the methods we have suggested earlier in this book will aid concentration. If our mind wanders, we ought gently to return to prayer as soon as we notice what has happened, trying not to be annoyed with ourselves. Sometimes we can bring the subject to which our mind wandered into our conversation with God. It is worth asking ourselves whether God is actually using our inability to concentrate to free us from our own rigid agenda for prayer. He may want to talk about what our mind drifted toward.

However, failure to concentrate can sometimes be distressing. If we forget about mental and intellectual discipline, and think in terms of interpersonal relationships, we can see how a lover will feel badly if he keeps forgetting that his beloved is with him, ignores her, and starts thinking about something entirely different. We do precisely this with God, and, not surprisingly, feel guilty when we notice what has happened. This is no excuse, but it may help to recall that the greatest saints have all had this same difficulty. Even the Apostles fell asleep when Jesus asked them to pray with him in Gethsemane. Remember also that we are held secure by God's great love for us; we are not attached to him by the frail thread of our concentration. Probably the only cure for this difficulty is continuing practice. As we grow in the awareness of God's love for us, as we get to know him better, and as we become accustomed to conversation and communion with him, we shall discover that instead of finding it difficult to remember his presence for a little while, it becomes hard to forget his presence at any time.

Praying is made more difficult by interruptions, distractions, and competition. We cannot eliminate all distractions all of the time, but we can seek to minimize them most of the time. The times and places we choose for prayer should be reviewed if we find that the outside world persistently interferes with our prayer. If our problem is with interruptions from the telephone, the door bell, or people who live with us, we are almost certainly able to find a solution. We may have to go to bed earlier in order to wake up fresh and early before the telephone and door bell start ringing. We may have to witness to our family or friends that we need the time for uninterrupted prayer. Ignoring the telephone or insisting on being undisturbed is easier if you believe that you have a right to time for yourself for prayer; and it is easier to claim that right when you hold the conviction that prayer is the divine purpose, not a human luxury. God expects us to find the time.

Competition from other demands does more than interrupt the time given to prayer, it also challenges the allocation of time. Many of us live with very insistent pressures, and if prayer becomes one more source of stress as we struggle to fit it into our overloaded schedules, we shall risk resenting prayer. When we face this difficulty directly, we see that it is a question of our priorities and commitment. Does God come first or not? If God is first, then it is possible to find time for prayer. Something else might have to be cut out, but prayer is safe. This will require determination and sometimes ingenuity, but we cannot say that it is impossible when it is merely difficult. One of the greatest prayers was offered when the nails were being driven into Jesus's hands. Prayer is always possible, even under the worst conditions.

Embarrassment is another difficulty. We may be ashamed to admit that we pray, and as a result make difficulties for ourselves by hiding our prayer time from other people. If we are secretive about prayer, it is harder to protect time and have others respect it. I have been fascinated to hear soldiers talk quite freely about praying in battle. Perhaps, because they have proved themselves, they are confident that no one will accuse them of weakness, and their manliness will not be threatened by the admission that they prayed. A partial explanation for our reluctance to come out of the closet as people who pray, is that we do not like the sickening piety and cant of some who parade their prayerfulness for all to see. It was because of this that Jesus sent us into the closet and told us not to show off our prayer lives. But if we carry this reserve to the point of being ashamed, we fail to witness as we ought to the importance of prayer for every Christian.

Loneliness in private prayer is almost an inevitable difficulty. In corporate prayer and worship we join other Christians. The kind of prayer we are discussing in this book is done when we are alone. However, we ought not to allow it to become a lonely activity. First, we are not alone in prayer because we are with God. Secondly, there is strictly no such thing as an individual Christian alone at prayer. We always pray as members of the Church community, and our voice is part of an enormous volume of prayer continually offered to God. Notice that even when we are physically alone we often pray in the plural, saying, for example, "*Our* Father." We are praying together even when we forget that we are doing so.

In spite of knowing these truths we may still feel lonely. This may be because we never, or too rarely, talk about prayer with any other Christian. If we have chosen a spiritual guide or friend, then we have made sure of at least one other person with whom we can share our experience. It would greatly enrich Church life if we would all loosen up a little and be more open in our discussions with each other about things that really matter. Failing a sudden explosion of heart to heart talks in your parish, you may have to take the risk of initiating a conversation about prayer with a friend, or with a fellow parishioner whom you feel might become a spiritual friend. As a parish priest for many years I have learned that lots of people pray, but you could know them for years and not discover anything about their experience. Many feel like Elijah that they are the only one left (1 Kings 19:14). Others more probably feel that they do not have much to offer in the way of insights and keep quiet, undervaluing the progress they have already made. This is the great untapped resource for contemporary spirituality. We could learn a great deal if we would share our experience with each other. In this process we would also overcome our spiritual loneliness.

It is difficult to pray in a society and culture that do not take prayer seriously. If prayer is a marginal or minority activity in a community, it is harder to do than it would be in a community where it was central and practised by the majority. Our overall culture is very secularized. Unless we are identified with a spiritual community with its own culture that values and practises prayer, we shall find that the attempt to pray demands a heroic struggle. We are not to withdraw from God's world, and by continuing to belong to the wider culture we contribute to its transformation with the resources we have discovered through our Church life. But secularization today could almost destroy individual prayer if spirituality were not sustained in the life of the Church. We overcome the social and cultural pressures of secular society through active participation in the fellowship of the Church.

Lack of personal discipline will make it difficult for us to pray. The evidence of human experience supports the view that although prayer is a simple activity in itself, it demands a daily discipline of practice. We shall flounder and be dissatisfied if we only try it occasionally. Furthermore we can go for long periods without experiencing any emotional or other discernible rewards for praying; so only our faithfulness can keep us going. Many of us not only lack discipline, but also resent any suggestion that we need it in what we regard as the private area of our lives. We feel over-organized and pushed around in the public arena and fight to protect a private space in which we may please ourselves unhampered by rules. There is a social and spiritual sickness behind this attitude, and all we can do here is insist that spiritual growth requires internal discipline. To progress in prayer we shall need to be determined. It is an evasive excuse to say that we do not expect a love relationship to follow a program and that there is no point in praying unless you feel like it. Your love affair with God will wither unless you regularly find the time required to nurture it.

This problem is largely solved when we establish new habits. Most of us have some kind of rhythm to our lives. If our established rhythm does not include prayer, we shall find it difficult to insert it like an extra step into a dance without getting the beat confused. We may need to take several months and try different patterns of times and styles of prayer before we discover the right rhythm for our lives. Then we shall need to persevere until our natural lifestyle includes prayer.

It is bad enough to want to pray and discover that we are too disorganized or undisciplined to be regular about it; it is far more devastating to lose all desire to pray. This is not merely a matter of not feeling like praying on an off day, but a radical questioning of the whole enterprise. We may feel that God has let us down and is not really present with us in prayer. Or we may doubt the reality of God and conclude that prayer is pointless. Perseverance in prayer always remains the correct course of action. This is not the time to worry about being a hypocrite. I am not the only Christian who has proved to himself that it is better to continue praying even when feeling like an atheist and suspecting that the exercise is nonsensical and futile. In one difficult period I came across the doggerel verse:

> The man who once so wisely said,
>   Be sure you're right, then go ahead,
> Might well have added this, to wit,

Be sure you're wrong before you quit.

(*Expository Times* LXXV. 3. p. 96)

Even if we lose the desire to pray, we ought to keep on praying. This is not hypocrisy; it is steadfastness. God will understand even though we do not.

Many difficulties with prayer originate in our sinfulness. These problems cannot be solved by methods and techniques of prayer, but only be repentance and forgiveness. The obstacle to communion with God can no longer be described as sin in itself. Christ has overcome that obstacle. Clearly also sinners often pray without any difficulty at all. Problems occur when we are reluctant to repent; it is not that we have sinned but that we are unwilling to change our lives and let go of our sin. For example, if we refuse to love and forgive each other, then we oppose ourselves to the divine love. Because it brings us into intimate contact with God's holiness, prayer will change our lives. If we resist the change, we are cutting the relationship. Prayer cannot be kept separate from life. So we cannot enjoy a pleasant relationship with God in private but refuse to alter our behaviour in public. In stating the problem we have pointed to the solution. In prayer we repent and turn to God, and in prayer he forgives us and makes us like himself. But he will not force us; we must let it happen.

We ought not to define sin too narrowly. In the love relationship of prayer we do not encounter difficulties because God turns nasty when we are naughty. The problem is more to do with the mingling of our natures. We are to be caught up into the divine life. Sin keeps us earthbound. Any sin will do this. The difficulties do not only arise from what the world would call wickedness. Things that seem harmless or even good in themselves can interfere with our relationship with God and therefore spoil our communion in prayer. For example, any attachment may become a problem. Saint John of the Cross writes:

It makes little difference whether a bird is tied by a thin thread or by a cord. For even if tied by thread, the bird will be prevented from taking off just as surely as if it were tied by cord — that is, it will be impeded from flight as long as it does not break the thread. Admittedly the thread is easier to rend, but no matter how easily this may be done, the bird will not fly away without first doing so. This is the lot of a man who is attached to something; no matter how much virtue he has he will not reach the freedom of the divine union.

(The Ascent of Mount Carmel, Book 1,11:4. p.97, from *The Collected Works of S. John of the Cross* trans. by K. Kavanaugh and O. Rodriguez. I.C.S.

Publications, Institute of Carmelite Studies, Washington, 1979).

We often find prayer to be a painful process. Sometimes it is agony. Part of the problem this poses can be answered by asking whether the pain would be less without prayer. For example, would Jesus' agony in the Garden have been greater or less if he had faced it without prayer? When we must deal with a painful experience, facing it in communion with God is in fact a help. Even when it is the honesty of our prayer that makes us confront a painful reality, the pain is still not caused by prayer but alleviated by it. Because part of our real lives is involved in bitterness and darkness, realistic prayer cannot be all sweetness and light, although the overall direction of prayer is from darkness to light. Some of the pain we experience in life would be worse without prayer.

There is, however, a pain that seems to belong to the process of prayer itself. Many Christians recount a personal spiritual history that begins with a stage of enthusiasm and warmth when prayer is very rewarding. This is followed by a long period when there seem to be all difficulties and no rewards. It is like being lost in a dark mine, worse even than a tunnel where one can see at least a glimmer of light at the end. This can be confusing, depressing, and very painful. I do not know how much of this process is the inevitable result of our alienation from God and is made necessary by the difficulty of transforming us. I am sure that it includes a process of weaning in which we are gradually set free from dependence on trivial rewards. For some reason we find it hard to grow to spiritual maturity. If we are to enter into communion with the living God, we have to lose our childish idol. We are blind to the vision of God when we repeatedly cling to a sentimental or superstitious notion of a god who responds to our manipulation. Some people, it must be admitted, do not seem to have a superstitious idol to forsake, and claim to have missed the enthusiasm and warmth of stage one. For them prayer has more often than not been a dark struggle. What some mystics call ''the dark night of the soul'' is not to be avoided or treated as a disease of the spiritual life. Rather it is a positive although painful process that leads toward our perfection. Knowing that it is to be expected can help us work through the process instead of seeking to escape from it. I hope you will not be discouraged to read that it is a process through which we may pass more than once. For most of us spiritual growth does not proceed as a straight line of ascent.

Difficulties in prayer would defeat us if prayer were merely a human activity. Thank God our companion in prayer is the Holy Trinity, whose grace is more than sufficient for us.

9   Effects of prayer

In learning to pray it is helpful to have some idea of what results we can expect. When we ask what prayer brings about, we discover that our answer can only include a part of what we believe may be happening. We cannot measure the results of prayer in the wider purposes of God; so we must be satisfied to discern in our personal lives the changes that come from our experience of prayer. Far more is accomplished than we can know.

There are some things that we can expect to happen with reasonable confidence. For example, when we pray, our sense of inner peace will grow over the long term. If something in our lives needs to be changed, we may experience temporary turmoil, but the overall result of prayer is harmony with God, harmony within ourselves, a good will that promotes harmony with others, and everything else that belongs to what the Bible calls *shalom* or peace. When we practise a quiet time and use contemplation or meditation, we learn to be still. A result of prayer is a growing stillness and tranquillity at the centre of our beings.

Communion with God leads to sharing his nature; therefore prayer leads to holiness and righteousness. This transformation of our lives is not accomplished overnight, but through prayer God does form us into new persons. Alienation from God is overcome in the reconciling activity of prayer. We shall also discover that instead of living fractured lives where one part of us is in conflict with the other, prayer integrates all dimensions of our being. Prayer leads to integrity.

Many people describe the effects of prayer in the language of liberation. They accept the discipline of regular prayer and discover a new freedom. United with God we are free from the bondage of our past; and death, sin, and fear can no longer tyrannize our lives. We cannot be free without power. Through prayer God provides us with the power that we need to be free, but that cannot be used to enslave others. Because the divine power is the power of love, it is always creative and liberating.

Another favourite way to describe the results of prayer is to talk about the discovery of meaning and purpose. In contemporary society people often feel like the victims of forces beyond their control, or they see themselves aimlessly drifting through a pointless existence. In prayer we enter into a covenant wth God to direct our lives in harmony with his purposes. We are on a journey to sanctity and the vision of God, and on the way we already encounter and communicate with God who is the end of the journey.

Part of what happens to us in prayer can be described as assimilation. Paul wrote to the Philippians,

"Whatever is true, whatever is honourable, whatever is just, whatever is pure, whatever is lovely, whatever is gracious, if there is any excellence, if there is anything worthy of praise, think about these things" (Philippians 4:8). We do this in prayer, particularly in meditation, and the result is that we assimilate these qualities. For example, if we meditate deeply about peace, we find that it becomes part of our inner being.

Closely linked with meditation is the process of pondering. Some of the mysteries that we consider in prayer defy our understanding. But instead of rejecting what puzzles us, we follow the example of the Virgin Mary and keep the mystery in our heart. There we turn it over, revolve it in our minds, treasure and guard it. If what we ponder is truly a mystery, we shall never solve it like a puzzle, but it will bear fruit in our lives. I do not think it is blasphemous to say that through this process in prayer the word of God is made incarnate in today's world. When we pray we can expect to become vehicles of the incarnation.

An extension of this incarnational understanding of prayer is to become aware that in prayer we experience the union of the two natures of Christ, the divine and the human. Saint Athanasius, the great defender of the doctrine of the Incarnation, said God became man that humanity might become God. This daring claim declares our destiny. It is possible because the divine nature is already united with our human nature in Christ. Through Christ, in prayer and sacraments, God accomplishes his purpose and unites us with himself. Although it is frightening to consider our deification, we must struggle to understand that a result of prayer will be our being drawn into closer and more perfect union with God.

Is this too great a claim to make for the effects of prayer? We cannot support it incontrovertibly from our own experience; but if we note the importance of prayer in the life of Jesus, and then examine the examples of the Blessed Virgin Mary, the saints, and holy persons throughout the ages, we can reach a moral certainty that in Christ's case prayer expressed, and in the other cases prayer led toward and nurtured, the union of our human nature with the divine. When we acknowledge that this is an effect of prayer, we can begin to look for ways in which it is already happening in our own experience of prayer.

We must admit that an improper use of prayer can be dangerous for us. For example, if we use the Jesus Prayer as it was used by the author of *The Way of the Pilgrim*, it could destabilize our whole lives. Some of us need shaking up, but we do not want to become mentally unbalanced. The psycho-technical method of prayer ought not to be used on its own, but only in the context of a full and balanced life in the Christian community, and preferably with a wise spiritual advisor. Psychological methods may leave us very vulnerable, and we can fall victim either to our own inner confusion or to manipulation and exploitation by unscrupulous charlatans.

The safeguard against this is to remain within the security of the orthodox family of the Church and to be sure that Christ is enthroned in our hearts. There are many esoteric methods and styles of prayer. Perhaps these may be safe for those who are experienced and secure in the life of prayer. For those of us who are beginners, we are wise to stay within the realiable tradition of trinitarian prayer. Trinitarian prayer is offered by us to the Father, through the Son, in the Spirit. Always address your prayer to God the Father, always approach him through the Son, and always do this in the power of the Holy Spirit. Similarly, in prayer the Father gives his presence, his love, his grace, and his nature to us through Jesus Christ, the Son, in the power of the Holy Spirit.

So long as the life of prayer follows this trinitarian way, we can experiment with different methods, techniques, and styles; and we can be daring, creative, spontaneous, and free. We shall also be safe, knowing that we are in conversation with God our Father and creator, who called Abraham and revealed himself to Moses and the prophets, and who sent his Son Jesus Christ into the world. We always meet him through Jesus Christ. The conversation could not happen unless the Holy Spirit was already within us and united with our spirit — or to put it the other way, unless we were already in the Spirit. We do not need to understand the meaning of these directions as we begin the path of prayer, but we need to follow them. The witness of faithful Christians throughout the ages is that this trinitarian way leads to the vision of God and union with the Alpha and the Omega, who is our beginning and our end.

Appendix

Adoration

Glory to the Father, and to the Son, and to the Holy Spirit: as it was in the beginning, is now, and will be for ever. Amen.

or

Blessed be God the Father, who created me,
Blessed be God the Son, who redeemed me,
Blessed be God the Holy Spirit, who sanctifies me,
Blessed be the Holy, undivided, and life-giving Trinity,
Three persons and one God for ever and ever.

or

Holy, holy, holy, Lord God almighty!
early in the morning our song shall rise to thee;
holy, holy, holy, merciful and mighty,
God in three persons, blessed Trinity!

Holy, holy, holy, Lord God almighty!
All thy works shall praise thy name in earth and sky and sea;
holy, holy, holy, merciful and mighty,
God in three persons, blessed Trinity!

(Reginald Heber 1783–1826, *The Hymn Book*, no. 50)

Penitence

Most merciful God,
we confess that we have sinned against you
in thought, word, and deed,
by what we have done
and by what we have left undone.
We have not loved you with our whole heart;
we have not loved our neighbours as ourselves.
We are truly sorry and we humbly repent.
For the sake of your son Jesus Christ
have mercy on us and forgive us,
that we may delight in your will
and walk in your ways,
to the glory of your name. Amen.
(*The Holy Eucharist*)

or

Grant, we beseech thee, merciful Lord, to thy faithful
people pardon and peace; that they may be cleansed
from all their sins, and serve thee with a quiet mind;
through Jesus Christ our Lord. Amen.
(*The Book of Common Prayer*, 1959, Canada, p. 252)

Petition and Intercession

Make your own list including concerns about your own life and
   the church
   the world
   all in authority
   the local community
   your family and friends
   those in need
   the departed

or

"The Prayers of the People" from *The Holy Eucharist* can easily be adapted for personal use.

Thanksgiving

Make your own personal list of thanksgivings; then recite a psalm, e.g.

Psalm 30 after recovery from sickness, or

Psalm 103 when particularly conscious of God's pardoning mercy.

or

use "A General Thanksgiving," *Book of Common Prayer*, 1959 Canada, p. 14.

or

Thanks be to thee, O Lord Jesus Christ, for all the benefits which thou hast given me; for all the pains and insults which thou hast borne for me. O most merciful Redeemer, Friend and Brother, may I know thee more clearly, love thee more dearly, and follow thee more nearly, day by day; for thine own sake. Amen.

(Saint Richard, Bishop of Chichester, AD 1197)

Dedication

After making a definite resolution you may wish to add a general act of commitment, e.g.

Suscipe domine

Take, O Lord, and receive all my liberty, my memory, my understanding, and all my will, all I have and possess. Thou hast given all this to me; to thee, O Lord, I restore it: all is thine, dispose of it entirely according to thy will. Give me thy love and thy grace, for this is enough for me.

(*The Spiritual Exercises of Saint Ignatius of Loyola*, trans. by W.H. Longridge, Mowbrays, p. 155)

or

O God, my Maker, help me today to live bravely, to act kindly, to speak truly. Help me to do my duty; Christ did; I want to be like him: help me to put work before pleasure, others before self, and none before thee; through Jesus Christ my Lord. Amen.

(I think I learned this from my vicar when I was fifteen; I have no idea where he found it.)

Make your own anthology. You may wish to include:

The Jesus Prayer

Lord Jesus Christ, Son of God, have mercy on me a sinner.

Veni, Creator Spiritus

Come, Holy Ghost, our souls inspire,
   And lighten with celestial fire.
Thou the anointing Spirit art,
   Who dost thy seven-fold gifts impart.

Thy blessed Unction from above
   Is comfort, life, and fire of love.
Enable with perpetual light
   The dullness of our blinded sight.

Anoint and cheer our soiled face
   With the abundance of thy grace.
Keep far our foes, give peace at home:
   Where thou art guide, no ill can come.

Teach us to know the Father, Son,
   And thee, of both, to be but One;
That, through the ages all along,
   This may be our endless song:
      Praise to thy eternal merit,
      Father, Son, and Holy Spirit.

(*Book of Common Prayer*, 1959 Canada, p. 653)

Soul of Christ, sanctify me;
Body of Christ, save me;
Blood of Christ, invigorate me;
Water from the side of Christ, wash me;
Passion of Christ, strengthen me.
  O good Jesu, hear me;
Within thy wounds hide me;
Suffer me not to be separated from thee;
From the malignant enemy defend me;
In the hour of my death call me;
  And bid me come to thee;
That with all thy saints I may praise thee
  For ever and ever. Amen.

An Obsecration before the Crucifix

Lord, by this sweet and saving sign,
Defend us from our foes and thine.
  Jesu, by thy wounded feet,
    Direct our path aright:
  Jesu, by thy nailed hands,
    Move ours to deeds of love:
  Jesu, by thy pierced side,
    Cleanse our desires:
  Jesu, by thy crown of thorns,
    Annihilate our pride:
  Jesu, by thy silence,
    Shame our complaints:

Jesu, by thy parched lips,
    Curb our cruel speech:
Jesu, by thy closing eyes,
    Look on our sin no more:
Jesu, by thy broken heart,
    Knit ours to thee.
Yea, by this sweet and saving Sign,
Lord, draw us to our peace and thine.
(Quoted by E. Milner-White in *A Procession of Passion Prayers*, p. 2, from the *Cuddesdon Office Book* 1940 edition).

Prayer of Saint Francis

Lord,
Make me an instrument of your peace.
Where there is hatred, let me sow love;
where there is injury, pardon; where there is doubt, faith;
where there is despair, hope; where there is darkness, light;
and where there is sadness, joy.
O Divine Master, grant that I may not so much seek to be consoled as to console; to be understood as to understand; to be loved as to love. For it is in giving that we receive; it is in pardoning that we are pardoned; and it is in dying that we are born to eternal life.

Hail Mary, full of grace, the Lord is with thee; blessed art thou among women, and blessed is the fruit of thy womb, Jesus. Holy Mary, Mother of God, pray for us sinners, now and at the hour of our death. Amen.